The Architects
of Rap

The Architects of Rap

Poison in Our Culture

Les Taha

Silverstone Press

About the author

Leslie Taha is an African American writer, social activist, and former syndicated cartoonist. His cartoons and commentaries have appeared in newspapers throughout the U.S. and Canada.

Silverstone Press
P.O. Box 8429
Tacoma, WA 98418

ISBN 0-9740710-0-5

LCCN 2003092587

To My Wife,
Chholing

Contents

Introduction

Throughout the years, African Americans have been portrayed in some pretty negative ways. Just reflect on some of the stereotypical images that were around in the mid- 1800s to 1900s.

And while most of us look back on those old stereotypes with utter disdain, how many of us realize that there are new stereotypes out there that are much worse than the old? Rap / hip-hop music, videos, magazines and so on, portray African Americans as being violence-prone, criminal, promiscuous and stupid. Not only do they attempt to define us in this image, but, even worse, they blatantly promote, glamorize, and glorify this type of behavior.

But this book isn't only about the poisonous elements laced into the hip-hop culture; it's really about the poisonous elements laced into the American culture in general.

It's about an "entertainment" industry gone mad, out of control, bombarding us all with immorality and decadence from every direction.

What follows is a satirical attack, not necessarily on a style of music that's being promoted, but rather a style of behavior that's being promoted.

It's Not the Music; It's the Words

Most people are attracted to rap / hip-hop music initially because of the music, not the words and images associated with it.

The problem with rap / hip-hop isn't really the music. Music is a good thing. Rap / hip-hop music, rock music, soul music, jazz, classical... It's all good.

The problem is the words and images that are woven into them. And in the case of rap / hip-hop we all are quite aware of what those words and images are: glorification of criminal behavior, promiscuity, drugs, and images consisting of the most ugly, most degrading black stereotypes.

The words and images are fused so tightly with the music that it seems like one entity. You hear the music and it conjures up the negative images in your mind, in a Pavlov's dog kind of way.

Without a doubt, **not** all rap / hip-hop music is like that. There are artists out there who have very positive messages in their music. This is not to say that all music must have a so-called "positive" message. Music doesn't have to have a message at all, but it definitely shouldn't have a negative message.

And the problem isn't really that **some** rap / hip-hop music contains negative messages (negative is putting it mildly).

The problem is that **most** rap / hip-hop that is promoted by the big music companies contains negative messages.

3

Yes, non-destructive rap / hip-hop is out there, but that's not what the big boys have **chosen** to promote. The negative, degrading, corrupting variety is what they are filling our airwaves with. And make no mistake about it: the big boys are the ones calling the shots, not the rappers.

Now some might say that all the bad stuff in it is what makes it so good, so original, so diverse, so creative, so cutting-edge.

In reality, the entertainment industry is selling us immorality disguised as creativity.

Vulgarity masquerading as originality.

Cultural degeneracy posing as cultural diversity.

Degrading stereotypes packaged as cutting edge.

Poison labeled as spice.

Originality, creativity, diversity, cutting edge are all very good things, and we need much more of it. But these very positive and wonderful things have nothing to do with those other things.

Good food is one thing; poison is another.

If I wanted to kill you, I might have a hard time trying to get you to eat a plate of pure rat poison. But if I laced your favorite food with it, you'd wolf it down and never know what hit you.

Let's keep the good food and lose the poison.

4

Old Stereotypes for New

We are all familiar with the old negative images and racial stereotypes of African Americans that once existed in this country.

I think everyone would agree that they were horrible, slanderous, misrepresentations of African American people.

Here are a few examples of the old stereotypes that can be found at the Jim Crow Museum of Racist Memorabilia:

"The brute caricature portrays Black men as innately savage, animalistic, destructive, and criminal -- deserving punishment, maybe death. This brute is a fiend, a sociopath, an anti-social menace."

"...the 'new issue (Blacks),' for the most part, are lazy, thriftless, intemperate, insolent, dishonest, and without the most rudimentary elements of morality....Universally, they report a general depravity and retrogression of the Negroes at large.."

"The Brute caricature depicts black men as angry, physically strong, animalistic, and prone to wanton violence..."

"...the Black birthright was 'sexual madness and excess'."

"... intellectually childlike, physically unattractive, and neglectful of their biological families."

"Blacks were, they argued, hedonistic children, irresponsible, and left to their own plans, destined for idleness – or worse…"

Those old stereotypes were pretty nasty, weren't they? But guess what? All those ugly old stereotypes are still with us. They're now embodied in the new, improved stereotypes that we find in rap / hip-hop.

The degrading stereotype depicting the Black man as the brute, the criminal, "prone to wanton violence"... isn't that Gangsta Rap?

The degrading stereotypes depicting Blacks as being hedonistic, childlike, immature, lacking in morals, irresponsible, prone to "sexual madness and excess"... Isn't that what we find in most rap / hip-hop music and videos?

Of course some African Americans do fit those stereotypical descriptions, then and now. But most African Americans do not fit those descriptions, then and now. That's the nature of a stereotype. The worst among a group is portrayed as the norm, or as an inherit trait of the group.

Now here is the thing that makes this new, improved stereotyping effort so deadly. Many African Americans actually **believe** this new stereotype about themselves. As a result, a distorted, slanderous stereotype is becoming a reality!

Isn't rap / hip-hop known as being "Black people's music"? Whenever a White person gets involved in rap / hip-hop and takes on those degrading attitudes and behaviors, isn't he referred to as "trying to be Black" or "acting Black"? Many people, Black and White, see the low behavior that we find in rap / hip-hop as being synonymous with "Black" behavior in general. How come decent and dignified behavior can't be identified as "Black" behavior?

Unfortunately the stereotypes are becoming a reality. The constant bombing of our community with these degrading images is taking its toll. It's having a very negative effect on us and our children.

It's like brainwashing. Think about it. Practically from day one, kids grow up listening to degrading stereotypes about themselves; stereotypes that cleverly define who they are to themselves without them even realizing it.

Don't you think that this can, and is, affecting them in their conscious and, especially, subconscious minds?

Do you know the devastating effects of growing up with a bad self-image lodged in your mind,
especially when that image of inferiority is lodged in your subconscious, where you can't readily analyze it. It lodges in your mind like a virus and "mysteriously" manifests itself in degrading, irresponsible, low, self-destructive behavior.

Have you heard the phrase, "You are what you eat"? Never have truer words been spoken.

When our children and adults constantly consume the mental foods of degradation, criminality, promiscuity, and irresponsibility, we will be made, to one degree or another, in that image.

We eat food laced with poison and then wonder what's killing us.

Does anyone honestly think that the African American community isn't being affected by this? Well, just hang on. Later in the book I'm going to give you some very shocking statistics.

No, I'm not saying that the destructive messages in rap / hip-hop are the cause of all of our problems. It is definitely a very big contributor, but it isn't the only cause. There are certainly historical factors involved. One generation builds upon the other. The laws of cause and effect are just as valid for the human world as they are for the inanimate world.

Maybe if more people realized that, we could have the same type of progress in the world of human relationships as we've had in the physical world, because if you keep following cause and effect, it will lead you to the ultimate cause of all things, which is the Creator. The implications of that are staggering, but that's another book. A big book.

Anyway, back to the subject. No, the destructive, degrading, messages in most rap / hip-hop are not the cause of all our problems, but they are certainly contributing and keeping us from getting back on our feet. It constantly jabs at and re-infects old wounds. And it creates new wounds. All this helps to keep us down.

It helps to keep us down in a big way because our ascent, contrary to popular talk, must begin within us, not outside of us. It begins much more with internal development than external development. And that is where we are being attacked, in the area most crucial to our ascent as a people.

Yes, this new stereotyping vehicle is indeed most insidious. It makes us an active participant in our own degradation. We become the inmate and the prison guard; the slave and the slave master.

Let me tell you, there are Black people out there who would fight you tooth and nail if you criticized rap / hip-hop. They'd defend it to their dying breath.

And don't let a White person criticize it. Man, they'll come at you with the fury of a thousand angry warriors.

There are some who have become so brainwashed that to criticize even the degrading parts of rap / hip-hop is, in their minds, the same as criticizing them. They take it very personally. They take it as a slap to the race. Why? Because they've eaten the good with the bad; the food with the poison. And they saw those opposing things as one entity. And the poison has gone to work on them.

In their subconscious they believe the stereotypes. Swallowed the whole thing, hook, line, sinker, fishing pole, the pier, everything. They have let someone else define who they are, – to themselves.

So what do we call one who has been totally brainwashed by the slave master, thinks the way he's told to think, act the way he's told to act? Isn't that an Uncle Tom?

It's the new Uncle Tom, who's actually much worse than the old. The old was physically a slave, and he didn't have many options. The new one can't claim that excuse.

Does anyone honestly believe that the words and images in rap / hip-hop aren't part of a nasty new stereotype that's adversely affecting African Americans?

There are certainly plenty of people out there who defend it.

Hmmm... maybe I should think about this some more.

You know, on the other hand... maybe it's not a stereotype.

Maybe it's real!

Wow! What a thought! Maybe the reason African Americans were portrayed the way they were in the past and in the present isn't because of some so-called stereotype. It's because that's the way we really are!

That's what the rappers are saying, isn't it?

When anyone criticizes the degrading stuff in rap, don't the rappers say that they're only reflecting reality?

Wow! It's not a stereotype – it's real!

And didn't "they" do some kind of scientific test once that proved that Black people was naturally more *stupider* than Whites?

Wow!

Well, I guess that clears it up. It's not a degrading stereotype. It's real.

Boy… this book didn't turn out quite the way I thought it would, but you can't argue with "science".

Oh well, I think I'll go play my harmonica, and eat some watermelon now.

The End.

Okay, back to reality.

I think we know that throughout history you'll find instances of one people attempting to put down another by clothing their racism in pseudo-scientific babble.

Jews, Asians, Native Americans, Irish Americans, Polish Americans have all been charged, at one time or another, with some type of "natural" defect. Of course once the people in question improved their condition, the former "scientific fact" of their genetic inferiority seemed to mysteriously disappear.

14

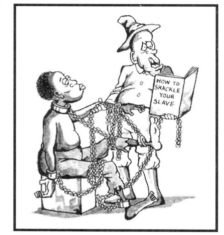

16

17

18

19

20

22

Little boy style shirts....

Revealing female apparel to
promote breeding...

26

A Man or A Boy

What is the definition of a man? I think most of us would agree that it goes way beyond the biological definition.

When we speak of attaining manhood, being a man, acting like a man, the best definitions strongly imply possessing attributes such as responsibility, fidelity, honesty, intelligence, internal strength, and dignity.

All right, here's a test.

Which of the following would you say is the best definition of a man?

Man #1 He's a responsible person, works hard, strives, treats women with dignity and respect, he's intelligent, takes care of his family, sets a good example, and is an asset to his family and community.

Man #2 Just the opposite of man #1. He's irresponsible, disrespectful of women, promiscuous, stupid and silly; he runs out on his kids and is basically a drain on his community.

Okay, that was an easy test. I think we all agree that man #1 is definitely the best example of what a man is.

Man #2 is essentially the opposite of a man. A "man" that behaves like the opposite of a man is a sissy. Sure he might be 6'6", 280 pounds of muscle and screws every woman in sight, but he's definitely a sissy if he behaves the opposite of a man.

Another way to put it would be to say if you're not a man, you're still a boy. **A little boy**.

During slavery and well into the post-slavery days, African American males were commonly referred to as boys. A twenty-year-old White man would address a 65-year-old Black man as "boy". "Hey, boy!" "Come here, boy". "Where you going, boy?".

African Americans really resented that then, and we really resent it now. What a degrading way to address a man!

But how are the new stereotypes in rap / hip-hop portraying Black males?

As boys. Little boys.

The exact opposite of a man. That is what's blatantly glorified and promoted in most rap / hip-hop music and videos.

I want to say that again.

The exact opposite of a man. That is what's blatantly glorified and promoted in most rap / hip-hop music and videos.

So, guess what? We're secretly being called "boy" again.

But this time it's so much more effective than before. It's oh-so- clever.

In the old days, a White man might call a Black man a boy to his face, and the Black man might resent it, but depending on the environment he was in at the time, he might have to just drop it, even though he resented it.

But now we have the new, improved racism.

In the new version, you'll never, ever, be called "boy" to your face. Oh no. The way it's done now is to fill the airwaves with stereotypical images that call you "**boy**", louder, clearer, and more effectively than they ever could before.

And the beauty of it is that this time you don't resent it! On the contrary, you believe it! They've successfully defined you to yourself, and it's all taking place in a nice safe location: your subconscious.

Just imagine millions of kids being constantly bombarded with these stereotypical images from the age of, say, four years old. Don't you think that might have a negative effect on them?

Maybe you, the reader, have survived the bombs, but do you think it's not taking its toll in the African American community? Just look around you. I'm seeing lots and lots of casualties.

I find it interesting that even the style of hip hop dress that's being promoted for men is the types of clothing that has traditionally been associated with things little boys would wear. It's almost like someone is playing an inside joke on us.

Now, I want to make something clear. What I'm writing about is definitely **not** a White vs. Black thing. I don't mean any of this in a "See what the White people are doing to us" kind of way at all.

There's only a relative handful of very clever "marketers" at the top of the food chain that are responsible for this. And their race doesn't matter. White, Brown, Black, Green, Plaid, Mauve, whatever. The point is that it's got to stop, and African Americans certainly are not the only victims of this. The moral poison in rap / hip-hop is only part of a much larger problem that's affecting us all.

Our New Enemy

What are the enemies of African Americans? At one time in our history, we could clearly say racism and oppression of the physical variety.

Yes, slavery was at one time our number one enemy. A little after slavery ended, racism, discrimination, and oppression were our biggest enemies. The psychological, cultural, and economic after-effects of slavery were (and still are) a serious problem for us.

But today, contrary to popular belief, racism, discrimination, and oppression are not our biggest enemies anymore; not by a long shot. I'm not saying they should be taken completely off the list, but there are much bigger enemies that have risen to the top.

So what's at the top of the list now?

Broken families, "playerism", immoral behavior, spiritual weakness, criminality, lack of education, substance abuse: these are our top enemies today.

Also on our list of enemies is the lack of a good economic base, better schools, better jobs, more African American-owned businesses, more property ownership, and a stronger political voice.

You'll notice that the first part of the list consists of things related to our own internal development as individuals and families.

The second part is composed of things related to community development.

The first part is by the far the most important. It's what leads to attaining the second part of the list. Without a doubt, what we need most is internal development and strong families. It begins there and then works outward to produce a strong community, economically and politically. Not the other way around.

Not to sound contradictory, but economic and political development can also help to stimulate individual and family development. They work together. It's important to work on both fronts. The internal helps develop the external and the external can help develop the internal, but the more important of the two, without a doubt, is the internal.

The after-effects of slavery are seldom talked about, but remain a very big problem. That was our starting point (what a way to start), and it's still manifesting itself in many negative ways.

Once again, the laws of cause and effect are just as valid for humans as they are for inanimate objects. Wherever you are now, if you retrace your steps, it will explain how you got there.

I know slavery may seem like ancient history, but it's not.

My father was 58 years old when I was born, and when he was a kid, all the old people had been slaves when they were young. I remember him casually talking to my uncles and aunts about it, and as a kid, I would casually listen, but when I got older and reflected on it, it hit me! I'd think, man! When my father was a boy, all the real old people had been slaves when they were young!

The effect of slavery on African Americans is certainly a book unto itself; a very big subject that's way beyond the scope of this book

But saying that the effects of slavery are currently a big problem for African Americans is not making excuses. It's stating a fact. And that fact puts the ball squarely in our court. That fact says, okay, slavery is over and it has done its damage. So whose responsibility is it to repair the damage? It's primarily our responsibility.

It's like tracing serious problems in your adult life back to serious problems in your childhood. You should use it as a way to correct your current problems, but you certainly should never use it as an excuse to keep behaving the same way.

We have to heal, but guess what— there are things out there that are hindering our healing, jabbing at the wounds, re-infecting them, and creating new wounds.

Things that jab, hinder, and cripple our internal and family development are big, big enemies. We're being bombed and it's producing casualties all around.

Here are some very interesting statistics.

Unwed Mothers

According to the U.S. National Center for Health, in 1999, 68.9% of all African American infants were born to unwed mothers, compared with 26.8% for Caucasian infants. In 1963 the figure was 23.6% for African American infants and 3.1% for Caucasian infants.

A 2001 U.S. Census survey showed that only 38% of African American children live in a two-parent home, compared with 78% for Caucasian children.

A 1996 U.S. Census survey showed that only 30.4% of African American females are married, compared to 56.6% of Caucasian females.

The 1996 Progress of Nations Report produced by UNICEF states:

"The steep rise in solo-parent families began in the 1960s, and long-term studies are beginning to reveal the consequences. The most obvious result is a rise in mothers and children living in poverty. In the US, a child living in a solo-mother family is five times as likely to live below the national poverty line, as defined by the Luxembourg Income Study."

A census brief from the U.S. Department of Commerce states that 69% of children raised by never- married women live near or below the poverty line.

What the above clearly illustrates is an economic problem stemming from a behavioral problem. But none of us **really** wants this. Without a doubt, most single mothers would prefer to have strong, committed husbands.

Single motherhood is a big problem for the African American community. There are more broken homes now than there were during slavery. It's a problem not only economically, but in other ways as well. Children from single parents are more likely to get involved in crime, more likely to be incarcerated, more likely to abuse drugs and alcohol, less likely to go to college, and more likely to become single parents themselves.

So what do you think of an "entertainment" industry that promotes, and glorifies, promiscuity and "playerism" to a people with big problems such as these?

What would you think if you saw a man on fire, and another man was spraying him with gasoline?

Well, that's us. We are a people on fire, and the "entertainment" industry is spraying us with gasoline.

Crime

According to the U.S. Department of Justice, although African Americans make up only 12.9% of the total U.S. population, they make up 46% of the prison population and 49% of the jail population.

The report also states:
"Based on current rates of incarceration, an estimated 28% of Black males will enter State or Federal prison during their lifetime, compared to 16% of Hispanic males and 4.4% of White males".

Twenty-eight percent? Is this outrageous? Is this alarming? It certainly should be.

The stereotype is becoming a reality. We are becoming slaves once again; not only mentally, but physically as well.

Private prisons (yes, private) have proliferated at a rate of around 900% over the last ten years.

These prisons are owned by private corporations that utilize prison labor to manufacture goods. Since their labor costs are practically nothing, they are highly profitable.

As of this writing, there are approximately 158 private "correctional" facilities in the U.S. with a total stated capacity of around 123,000. If they continue to grow at the current rate, by the year 2013, they'll be approximately 1,107,000 inmates (over half the current prison population) in private, for profit, corporate prisons.

So it looks like we've come full circle. It's back to the plantation... the corporate prison plantation.

So what should you think of an "entertainment" industry that promotes the type of rap / hip-hop that glorifies and glamorizes the thug life—criminality, criminal behavior, criminal attitudes—to a people with a serious crime problem?

Once again, we are a people on fire, and the "entertainment" industry is spraying us with gasoline.

Yeah, I know it's boring. That's cause it ain't nothin to do no more. Back in the old days, we used to hunt Blacks down, beat 'em up, ridicule 'em, kill 'em, but now they're doing it all to themselves.

Who Controls Hip-Hop

Some say that rap / hip-hop is Black people's music, but I can tell you for certain, Black people are not the ones controlling it. It's kind of strange to claim something is yours when you have no control over it.

As of this writing, there are five giant music companies that dominate and control the music business. They are Universal Music Group, Warner Music, Sony Music Group, BMG, and EMI. Operating through several hundred subsidiaries and over a thousand labels, these five companies, according to Nielson SoundScan figures, control approximately 86% of the U.S. and world music market, and all but EMI are part of even larger global entertainment conglomerates.

These companies have the resources, the capital, the manufacturing, marketing and promotional machinery, the channels of distribution, a virtual lock on the airwaves, and the strategic connections. In a nutshell, it all boils down to money, power, and knowledge. Those who have it have the control.

And there's a lot more to the entertainment industry than just recording companies. Radio stations, television stations, movie studios, television networks, cable and satellite companies, print media, all of these and more are part of the package.

How much of this do Black people control?

Sure, you see a lot of young, Black faces out front, but believe me, rap / hip-hop is controlled by fat, old, rich guys in expensive suits who prefer to stay behind the scenes.

No, the cultural gatekeepers in the entertainment industry didn't "create" the poisonous variety of rap / hip-hop, they **chose** it.

But we shouldn't get hung up on the race thing. That would be a major diversion from the problem that the guilty ones would love us to take.

Let's say that African Americans **are** the ones running the whole show, everything from top to bottom. Would it really matter? No. The problem isn't the race of the perpetrators; the problem is the poison that they're lacing into our culture.

Of course the entertainment industry will say that all they are doing is filling a market demand for their product.

I agree with that. A drug dealer is also just filling a market demand for his product when he sells heroin to your kids. Neither one of them cares about the tremendous harm their product does. They are both only concerned about profits.

So I guess that makes it all okay.

They both not only respond to a market demand, they also create demand. When your fifteen-year-old daughter becomes addicted to drugs, a market has been created. And that's good for business as far as the drug dealer is concerned.

The same holds true for the poison the entertainment industry sells us. It's good for business when we accept and crave it. Morality is definitely bad for business for the drug dealers and the "entertainment" dealers.

If some people drink alcohol long enough, pretty soon they'll crave it, even though it may be destroying their lives and their families. They'll crave what clearly harms them.

That also holds true for what we ingest into our minds. If you're raised on a diet of immorality, you'll certainly acquire a taste for it, even though it is harming you, your family, and your community.

Yes, there is a lot of music out there that hasn't been laced, but the balance is tipped heavily in favor of the laced variety, especially when it comes to rap / hip-hop. They don't have to give you a plate of 100% strychnine to kill you; they only have to lace your food with enough of it to do the job.

The things that get promoted are the things that sell, period. Yes, there are exceptions, but without a doubt, this is the way it works. If this weren't the case, why would billions of dollars be spent year after year to promote and advertise products?

The recording industry, in reality, is a shared monopoly, not a free market. As a result, a handful of powerful people set the agenda because they have the power and the purse. This isn't a theory; it's a fact of life. Money, knowledge, and power run the show. But should we just lie there and let them run us over like a freight train?

This is the story of J. P. Swifty, the owner of CMI (Castration Music Inc.) and one of the "visionaries" behind what is popularly known as rap / hip-hop music.

One day Swifty went out in search of another rap group to promote.

His search was very meticulous. He needed just the right group of individuals that in his mind would serve as, "the voice of Black America"

He went about his search in his usual manner, checking with various agencies to find the top notch talent he needed.

Swifty searched........

and searched......

and searched......

and searched......

and searched......

and searched......

Swifty eventually found the group with all the qualities he was looking for, and thus was born...

"The New Jack Stereotypes"

Swifty has big plans for the New Jack Stereotypes. He also dreams of one day selecting the most talented member of the group and promoting him as a solo artist.

In response to criticism that the hip-hop groups that CMI promotes are lacking in social awareness, the company has just released a new "Black pride" video from the New Jack Stereotypes that reflects their "African heritage".

Instead of focusing on the great ancient civilizations of Africa, such as those that existed in Mali, Ghana, Egypt, Ethiopia, Numibia, Zimbabwe, and many others...

Swifty made a decision to have the video reflect a more western viewpoint.

The New Jack Stereotypes went on to become one of the most successful rap groups in the country...

...then one night, one of the members had a very disturbing dream.

He dreamt that he was the historic slave leader Nat Turner. He had just mounted a successful assault against the slave master, and was now leading the slaves off the plantation to freedom.

Then suddenly, he realized that he wasn't Nat Turner...

...He was really Uncle Tom, and instead of leading the slaves to freedom, he was leading them right back to the plantation.

Influence

At this point someone is bound to say, oh, lighten up, it's just harmless entertainment.

Were the degrading, slanderous stereotypes of African Americans in the past also just "harmless entertainment"?

Can some of us only see the things that harmed us in the past, but are completely blind to the things that are harming us now?

Does anyone honestly think that children and adults are not influenced by what is in their environment?

Here's a good example.

Why is it that those of us born in the United States just happen to speak English? Did we consciously choose it, or was it an accident, or what?

The answer is obvious. We speak English because we were born into an English-speaking environment. I guess the environment influenced us.

So does this "influenced by our environment" thing only hold true for the language we speak? Don't you think other things in our environment influence us?

You'd probably prefer that your children not hang out with criminals, perverts, and dope fiends, because they might be a bad **influence** on them, right?

So what about the criminals, perverts, and dope fiends inside your television, in your radio, in your CD player? Is it okay for your children to hang out with them?

Don't get me wrong; I'm not just blaming the parents. The forces against good parents are absolutely overwhelming. Parents are just a part of their children's environment; just a part of what can influence them. You'd have to lock your kids in the basement until they were adults in order to totally keep the poison in the environment away from them. And as the years go by, it seems like the cultural environment has more influence and the parents less.

The problem with the entertainment industry isn't that criminals, perverts, and dope fiends are **depicted** in music, movies, television, etc.

The problem is that those types of behaviors are **promoted, glamorized and glorified** in music, movies, television, etc., and especially in rap / hip-hop.

The problem is that reality is being severely distorted. Reality is being turned upside down. Very bad things are presented to us as good things. **This is the problem**. If bad things were presented as what they are—bad things—there wouldn't be a problem.

That doesn't mean that everything has to be turned into a corn-ball, nursery school level "morality" lesson either, because that also is a distortion of reality. Forced, dogmatic "morality" lessons aren't what we need.

That phony type of stuff actually plays into the hands of those that want to keep the poisonous stuff flowing, because it'll make you think, "is this the only alternative?" We don't need either of those extremes of false reality.

Personal Tastes and Universal Values

Some might say that it's really just a matter of "personal taste".

Well, there are personal tastes and there are universal values.

The Creator made us all different. He made us so that we all have different personal tastes, different likes and dislikes, and that's a really wonderful thing.

But the Creator also made us all the same when it comes to universal values.

Let's say you like putting catsup on your ice cream. You think it's delicious. I think it's disgusting. That's personal taste. Nothing wrong with that.

Let's say you like robbing and beating up old people. You think it's fun. I think it's horrible. That's a universal value, a value we should all have in common. Would you argue that it's okay to rob and beat up old people because you personally enjoy it? Should that behavior be defended under the guise of "personal taste"?

The poisonous, degrading, and destructive elements in rap /
hip-hop that are destroying our community cannot be
defended under the guise of "personal taste". That's clearly
in the arena of universal values.

Free Will

Well, what about "free will"?

Sure there's free will, but it's not as free as some might
think. Your environment can greatly influence the choices
you make. Your environment can shape your free will.

Although I have a free will, I grew up speaking English,
because the English-speaking environment was so strong.
My free will to choose a different language never even
came into play. Do you think our free will might be
influenced by other things in our environment?

We can't allow the environment to be filled with corruption
and then just chastise the free will when it chooses wrong.
A corrupt environment can corrupt the "free will".

Yes, our environment has a tremendous influence on us,
whether we acknowledge it or not.

Now just imagine millions of African Americans
consuming the degrading, immoral words and images in rap
/ hip-hop practically from the time they are born. Does
anyone honestly think that it won't have an influence on
them? Just look around you. The answer is obvious.

Influence is a very powerful thing indeed. Those that realize
this can control those that don't, without them even
knowing it.

The New Black Hero

CMI 's subsidiary CCI (Castration Cinema Inc.) has decided to make a movie about Rodney the Rapper, one of the members of the New Jack Stereotypes that was tragically struck down in his prime.

The movie will deal with issues that face Black Americans everyday such as poverty, crime, drugs, and of course racism.

The executives at CCI decided to make this movie about Rodney because they felt his story could serve as an inspiration to young Black males.

The movie begins by showing various events in Rodney's childhood that may have contributed to his developement as a future rap artist.

As a young man, Rodney was a shy and sensitive soul who had difficulty approaching women.

But he was a very ambitious young man who worked hard to better himself.

This scene show Rodney in his young adult years as a typical Black family man stopping by as he always does on the first of the month to spend some quality time with his wife and children.

In addition to being a family man, Rodney was also an enterprising young entrepreneur.

But the racist system intervened. Rodney was put out of business and thrown into jail for no other reason than the color of his skin.

Once Rodney was released from jail, he needed funds in order to reestablish his business. He approached several financial institutions, but was abruptly turned down.

In this touching scene, Rodney turns to his grandmother for the financial help he needs.

With those funds, he was able to reestablish his business.

But he didn't stop there. Rodney continued to expand his business, and beat his competition...

...by using a variety of very creative and innovative marketing methods.

But once he hit the big time, the racist system once again reared its ugly head.

In this poignant scene, reminiscent of the plight of his forefathers, Rodney attempts to break free of the White man's bondage to once again become a free man.

Rodney's luck took a turn for the better when he was discovered on a street corner by the owner of CMI.

Swifty made him a member of The New Jack Stereotypes which went on to become one of the greatest rap groups in history.

Fame and fortune never went to Rodney's head.
He didn't forget those who stood by him during the
lean years.

But one day
tragedy struck.

Rodney like so
many of our young
Black men was
struck down in his
prime

A monument was erected in his honor. Rodney, the beloved figure idolized by the Black youth of America will forever be known as a martyr, a legend, and one of the great figures in African American history.

Family

Why is family so important? It's important because it's the basic building block of society.

What would happen if you constructed a building using a bunch of weak bricks? The whole building would be weak and eventually it would fall. The African American community is weakened when our basic building blocks are weak.

Weak families produce a weak community, and the weak community manifests itself in the form of crime, drugs, poverty, unemployment, homelessness, and lack of development in the areas of education, business, culture, and politics.

The Reverend Dr. Martin Luther King realized long ago that in order to have a healthy community, we must have healthy families. Here are some quotes from a book he wrote in 1967 entitled, "Where Do We Go From Here: Chaos or Community."

"The shattering blows on the Negro family have made it fragile, deprived and often psychopathic. This is doubly tragic because nothing is so much needed as a secure family life for a people seeking to rise out of poverty and backwardness."

"History continues to mock the Negro today, because just as he needs ever greater family integrity, severe strains are assailing family life in the White community."

"In short, the larger society is not at this time a constructive educational force for the Negro."

Another insightful voice from the 60s was that of the four-term senator from New York, Daniel Patrick Moynihan. Here is an excerpt from an article he wrote in 1965 for the Jesuit journal "America".

"From the wild Irish slums of the nineteenth-century Eastern seaboard, to the riot-torn suburbs of Los Angeles, there is one unmistakable lesson in American history: a community that allows a large number of young men to grow up in broken families, dominated by women, never acquiring any stable relationship to male authority, never acquiring any set of rational expectations about the future - that community asks for and gets chaos."

In 1965, Daniel Patrick Moynihan served as the Assistant Secretary of Labor for Policy Planning and Research. That year he released a very enlightening report entitled "The Negro Family: the Case for National Action." In the report he states:

"At the heart of the deterioration of the fabric of Negro society is the deterioration of the Negro family. It is the fundamental source of the weakness of the Negro community at the present time."

"There is probably no single fact of Negro American life so little understood by whites. The Negro situation is commonly perceived by whites in terms of the visible manifestations of discrimination and poverty, in part because Negro protest is directed against such obstacles, and in part, no doubt, because these are facts which involve the actions and attitudes of the white community as well."

"It is more difficult, however, for whites to perceive the effect that three centuries of exploitation have had on the fabric of Negro society itself. Here the consequences of the historic injustices done to Negro Americans are silent and hidden from view. But here is where the true injury has occurred: unless this damage is repaired, all the effort to end discrimination and poverty and injustice will come to little."

"The role of the family in shaping character and ability is so pervasive as to be easily overlooked. The family is the basic social unit of American life; it is the basic socializing unit. By and large, adult conduct in society is learned as a child. A fundamental insight of psychoanalytic theory, for example, is that the child learns a way of looking at life in his early years through which all later experience is viewed and which profoundly shapes his adult conduct."

The 1965 "Moynihan Report" showed, among other things, that 23.6% of all African American infants were born to unwed mothers. That rate is now at nearly 70%. His report also showed the relationship between the deterioration of the African American family and the many problems existing in the African American community.

Unfortunately, instead of seeing his report as a useful tool in combating our problems, many took a very defensive stance and rejected his findings, accusing him of "blaming the victim."

The Rev. Dr. Martin Luther King was **not** among those critics. His only reservation was not about the report itself, but on how some might try to misinterpret the problems found in it as being something inherent in African Americans, and thus a justification for discrimination.

The deterioration of the family is certainly not something exclusive to African Americans. White unwed motherhood has risen at a much faster rate than Black unwed motherhood over the last thirty years. The "Moynihan Report" showed that in 1963, 3.1% of White infants were born to unwed mothers. Currently, 26.8% of White infants are born to unwed mothers. So the percentage of White unwed mothers is now higher than what the percentage of Black unwed mothers was in 1963 when the report was released. Slavery gave African Americans a head start with this problem, but it looks like Caucasian Americans are quickly closing the gap. So this is clearly a problem that's common to all of us.

African American family problems started in slavery and are continuing today. Here are some more quotes from Dr. Martin Luther King's 1967 book, "Where Do We Go From Here: Chaos or Community."

"Today there is considerable discussion about the disintegration of the Negro family in the urban ghettos. We need only to learn something about the special origins of the Negro family to discover the root of the problem."

"The Negro family for three hundred years has been on the tracks of the racing locomotives of American history, dragged along mangled and crippled."

"On the plantation the institution of legal marriage for slaves did not exist. The masters might direct mating, or if they did not intervene, marriage occurred without sanctions."

"There were monogamous relationships, illegitimacies, abandonment and the repetitive tearing apart of families as children, husbands or wives were sold to other plantations."

"The Negro family is scarred; it is submerged; but it struggles to survive."

The continued destruction of our families is probably the biggest problem facing African Americans today. This is our present-day enemy. Shouldn't we attack this present enemy with the same zest and zeal as we did our past enemy, racial discrimination?

We need strong families. This should be at the forefront of our agenda. And when I say strong families, I mean family as defined as starting with a committed husband and wife.

There are those that are attempting to redefine the family. What we used to call "broken homes" or "broken families" is now being redefined as "family". The family is now being defined as anything and everything. Married people, unmarried people, single people, related people, unrelated people... whatever.

I know there are exceptions, but the traditional family consisting of a husband and wife is, without a doubt, much stronger than a broken family. These are the strongest bricks. These are the bricks we need to build our community.

So who should define what a family is? Nature. Nature has already defined that for us. All creatures, birds, bears, lions, wolves, humans, have a nature- defined family: the family that works best overall.

In the days of slavery (not that long ago), the slave master used to forcibly break up African American families for his own benefit.

Do we all agree that that was a horrible thing?

If we think that the breaking up of African American families was a horrible thing then, shouldn't we think of it as being a horrible thing now?

Or, if we use the new definition of the family that we have today, I guess we could say that the slave master didn't really break up any families.

He simply created new families.

Now here we are in the modern time and those that want to profit from us are still breaking up families.

But this time, his weapons of choice aren't ropes, chains, and whips. His new weapons are ultra-liberal ideas, and the promotion of "playerism".

We need strong building blocks to build a strong community, and this is what most of us truly want. Most single mothers would prefer not to be single mothers. I'm sure that most of them would love to have strong committed husbands. But there are major hindrances out there, pulling families apart and killing them before they even get started.

So what's the best way to break up the family? Create a break right where the family begins, with the man and woman.

In rap / hip-hop music we see the glorification and promotion of "playerism". Playerism is one of the African American community's biggest enemies because it stabs right at heart of where the family begins, with the man and the woman.

"Playerism" creates single mothers. "Playerism" creates animosity and distrust. "Playerism" creates divorce. "Playerism disrupts families. "Playerism" is the exact opposite of commitment. There is no real family without commitment. Am I a Player Hater? Yes I am.

We are constantly being bombarded with "playerism" and sexual images in an attempt to turn us into a community of dogs in heat, constantly on the prowl. Isn't it interesting that Black males are actually calling each other "Dogs" now?

Isn't the image of the irresponsible and promiscuous Black male one of those the ugly, degrading stereotypes that we hate people to label us with? Well, it looks like they're turning the stereotype into a reality.

Some might get defensive and accuse one of being anti-Black for pointing out serious problems in the African American family. Is it anti-Black to identify the very thing that's destroying us, the thing that's causing us so many problems?

Conversely, is it pro-Black to ignore it? Is it pro-Black to allow the modern day slave master to continue to bombard our community with destructive ideas for his own profit?

And I want to say again that these issues certainly are not exclusive to the African American community. The modern day slave master is bombing us all.

The History of CMI

Let's now take a quick look at the history of CMI

CMI is an old company with a very long and distinguished history. It began not as a music company, but as a trading company dealing in commodities.

After the Civil War, Swifty's great grandfather
decided that it was time to diversify the business.
He entered the entertainment field and began
promoting various Negro acts.

So as you can see, Swifty is just carrying on the grand traditions started by his forefathers.

Before getting into the music business, Swifty was involved in a number of other ventures.

Before actually entering the rap / hip-hop business, Swifty did very extensive research. He gathered ideas from all over the world that he could incorporate into his music business.

Swifty also hired the best choreographers he could find for CMI's hip-hop groups

Inside CMI

Let's now take a look at the various departments inside of CMI.

Song Writing Department

The lyrics to many of CMI's top hip-hop songs are composed by our very experienced group of staff writers.

CMI also gets songs from a number of freelance sources.

CMI receives valuable insights, direction, and suggestions from its team of in house creative consultants.

Marketing Department

The job of the marketing department is to first define the primary demographic group to be targeted...

...and then develop sophisticated marketing strategies to sell to them.

CMI sends its executives to innovative marketing workshops around the globe to learn new techniques of identifying, targeting, and capturing the consumer market.

Workshops on capturing the consumer market

Workshops on capturing market share

Sales promotion workshop

Quality Assurance

In order to maintain the quality of CMI's music, new rap / hip-hop songs are first tested on animal subjects.

They are then tested on human subjects in CMI's state of the art facility

During a recent stockholders meeting, Swifty concluded his presentation with a demonstration to graphically illustrate the effects of hip-hop on the African American male.

Research & Development

CMI also operates a research and development facility where staff scientists study the theory of how rap actually works.

Also, new more potent forms of rap are always being developed.

Merchandising Department

CMI's very profitable apparel division is constantly developing new rap / hip-hop clothing styles to market to African American consumers

CMI has also licensed a variety of products aimed at the children's market such as...

...Action Figures...

...Talking Dolls...

...and Breakfast Cereals

The Weapon of Ultra-Liberalism

Ultra-liberalism is the new vehicle that's being used to exploit us and consequently keep us down.

I'm not knocking liberalism itself. I believe that liberalism and conservatism both have more or less an equal amount of pros and cons. Even though the definition and attributes of the two are elusive and constantly shifting, I think that in order to have a healthy society, you'll need the proper balance of the best of both.

But this new ultra-liberalism weapon is something different. It's actually contrary to the ideals of most liberals and conservatives.

The very things that are the biggest enemies to African Americans (and all Americans) is sponsored, supported, and defended by ultra-liberalism.

The destruction of the family is an enemy of African Americans. Ultra-liberalism supports and defends it.

Promiscuous and irresponsible behavior is an enemy of African Americans. Ultra-liberalism supports and defends it.

Drug use is an enemy of African Americans. Ultra-liberalism supports and defends it.

The glorification of criminal behavior is an enemy of African Americans. Ultra-liberalism supports and defends it.

The death of true spirituality is an enemy of African Americans. Ultra-liberalism supports and defends it.

Even on the global level, the weapon of ultra-liberalism is taking its toll. So-called neo-liberal economics are creating vast disparities between the rich and the poor in the world. It's an integral part of the multinational corporate globalization plan.

Neo-liberal economics are not being used to create parity, or a level playing field, or a quasi-global economic democracy. Quite the contrary. Neo-liberal economics, under the **guise** of "free trade", "free markets", free this, free that (isn't that such a nice word, -"free"), are, in reality, creating vast disparity, very uneven playing fields, and something much more akin to a global economic dictatorship than a democracy. A global economic dictatorship also results in a global cultural dictatorship.

Ultra-liberalism robs people of the essential internal values that support them. In the form of neo-liberal economics, it's the new and improved colonialism that's very cleverly robbing people of their resources and labor.

What's the difference between an ultra-liberal and an old fashion racist?

Blacks just ain't got the brains that we's White people's got.

...another type of discrimination comes in the form of tests like this that are designed to be racially biased against Blacks.

...and the Black male is naturally promiscuweeous. They just lay around and breed, and make babies like a bunch of wild animals.

...and now we come to what is known in the vernacular of Blacks as, "the Player". The Player is the ultimate expression of Black manhood, masculinity, and virility.

...and you know them Blacks ain't nothin but a bunch of #@*%! criminals. None of them work. They'd rather steal than work.

...and in order to escape the sentence of poverty that has been imposed on them, we see here Black males joining together and pooling their collective talents as their only way of improving their economic predicament.

...and you know them Blacks is all on drugs, but I say go head, let 'em all kill themselves on drugs. That's one way to get rid of 'em.

...another argument in favor of the legalization of drugs is that this so-called, "war on drugs" is really nothing but a war against the Black community.

There's one good thing I can say about Blacks.
They does make some damn good entertainers.

The critics of hip-hop music should just lighten up.
Hip-hop is a Black art form that reflects the
realities of being Black.

White folks is just plain better than Blacks and that's that!

...and in my conclusion I say, who are we to judge. Who are we to say this is wrong, this is immoral, this is ignorant. To do so would be judging Black culture by White standards.

Censorship

At this point some may be wondering, "So what is the answer - censorship?

Those that want to continue to profit from the poison they're feeding us like to spook us with the idea of the dreaded - C word.

Censorship versus no censorship isn't really a legitimate question because, guess what, we've **always** had censorship.

But you know, censorship is such a nasty-sounding word. I think I'll stop using it. Let's replace it with another word that means the same thing, but sounds better. How about…"guidelines"?

Think about the history of newspapers, magazines, theater, movies and television and so on in this country. Has there ever been a time when they've operated completely without guidelines? Absolutely not.

And guidelines are something that we as Americans have always wanted. Can you imagine a situation where there were no guidelines at all?

What if the networks showed hard-core pornography during Saturday morning cartoons?

What if there was a television show that instructed viewers on how to rape and molest little children?

We'd be up in arms over something like that. Certainly no sane person would want the entertainment industry to operate completely without guidelines.

So the question isn't about whether we should have guidelines or not. We've always had them, and we've always wanted them. The question is where those lines should be drawn, and who's drawing them.

As far as who's drawing them, federal, state, and local governments draw some, but the big pen is in the hands of the industries themselves. They are generally supposed to govern themselves, but they're not doing a very good job of it, to put it mildly.

As the years go by, they keep moving the line, allowing more and more poison into our culture, and consequently into our minds.

Now they might try to argue that society has changed, that's why they keep redrawing the line.

Yes, society has changed, but what changed it? It was changed by those at the helm of our culture. When they redraw the cultural lines, it affects society.

So what was the original purpose of guidelines anyway? Wasn't the purpose to keep harmful things out of the culture that could adversely affect society?

It doesn't look like the entertainment industry is doing a very good job at self-policing. It reminds me of the time that my grandfather hired a bunch of wolves to guard his hen house. It didn't work out very well.

Okay, now we come to the "Well, if you don't like it, just turn it off" mantra. Yes, we should definitely turn it off, but that alone is far from solving the problem.

What if you lived in a country which was swimming in hard-core, dangerous drugs, and there were no laws against it, no police. And let's say that you're sane enough not to want your kids to become heroin or crack addicts while they're still in grade school.

Would you say that the only solution to that problem would be to tell your kids to "Just say no"?

The drug dealers would have a field day if that were the only solution put forth.

Does anyone think that alone would solve the problem, especially after the drugs have already corrupted the society? "Just say no" would be a joke without laws, and law enforcement.

It's the same with the "Just turn it off" philosophy. That by itself is very ineffective, and right now, our "cultural drug dealers" are having a field day.

That's like addressing the problem of air pollution by saying, "Just don't breathe it". The cultural pollution in our environment is thick, and it's impossible for us and our children not to breathe it.

What if animals acted like humans?

We have with us today, a distinguished panel of experts to tell us about their latest theories on the problems of parental over protectiveness.

Oh good, we can go out and graze now. The lions have offered to entertain the kids until we get back.

Man, this is some good stuff! You say the lions just gave it to you?

For the last time, yes! I assure you that this is the latest, hippest fashion. Now if you can just put this apple in your mouth...

I see old "Mr. Conspiracy Theory" is at it again.

Conclusion

I hope that I haven't given you the impression that I think we are all just innocent victims of the entertainment industry. I probably have, but I didn't mean to. There is another side to this.

Let's revisit the drug dealer analogy. The one who sells drugs is committing an illegal act, and the one who buys drugs is also committing an illegal act.

Do you think it would make any sense for law enforcement to concentrate all their efforts only on the seller of the drugs, and completely ignore the buyer of the drugs?

Of course not. Both are guilty. Perhaps the seller is a little "more guilty" than the buyer, but you could hardly call the buyer an "innocent victim".

It's the same with the sellers and buyers of cultural poison. The focus of this book just happens to be more on the seller than the buyer.

It's very important that we become aware of the negative influences in our cultural environment which are contributing to so many of our problems. So often you'll find those that love to lament about the effects of a problem, but never want to investigate the source of a problem.

If you trace the causes of most of our problems as African Americans (and all Americans), you'll land smack dab in the moral arena. The moral arena? How un-cool; how unsophisticated.

Many want to talk about political and economic solutions, but drive a wide berth around morality or, God forbid, true spirituality.

But this is the source of our strength. This is what keeps us from being susceptible to the poisonous influences. Throw that away and you've thrown away your protection.

Let me put a little footnote here. There's such an incredible abundance of phony, fake, hypocritical spirituality that I sometimes find it hard even to use the word, because it's been so tainted. So, in a way, one could hardly blame people from being turned off by it. But even though the religious world is ill and has been ill for some time, true spirituality does exist, and there are even some examples of it out there, but it is certainly harder to find than the common variety.

Yes, I definitely believe that political and economic solutions can play a big part in solving our problems, but the internal, moral factors are much more important, and if you neglect that, political and economic solutions will fall flat.

We must demand that the entertainment industry stop bombarding us with corruption. They are the gatekeepers of our culture, and they're seriously abusing their responsibility.

The airwaves to our minds are supposed to belong to us, but they are instead controlled by a few corporations. They have a very powerful concession, a shared monopoly in which they are essentially accountable to no one but themselves. That's what I call a dictatorship. I'd prefer a true, free market democracy.

There needs to be true competition, a true free market in the entertainment industry. What we have now is only a facade of a free market. Yes, there are a lot of entertainment choices out there, but the general tone, agenda, and direction is set by the few power players that dominate.

The timeless, borderless, universal values are the solutions to our problems: the values of obedience to our Creator; honesty; decency; family; fidelity; intelligence; and hard work. The values that were imparted to us from all the great Prophets of all revealed religions.

Our major influence should come from the best in our spiritual roots: the best in Judaism, the best in Christianity, the best in Islam, and other revealed religions - this is what should influence us most.

When we throw that away as the major influence in our lives, a slick operator always comes along and steps into that role.